School Screamers

Written by Ken Ross
Illustrated by Phil Garner

This book is MINE
This boot another.
Don't touch the first
For fear of the other.

HENDERSON
PUBLISHING PLC

©1995 HENDERSON PUBLISHING PLC

9 A.M. MONDAY MORNING - GROAN

HOMEWORK - HILARIOUS (NOT...)

ONTO THE SPORTS PITCH

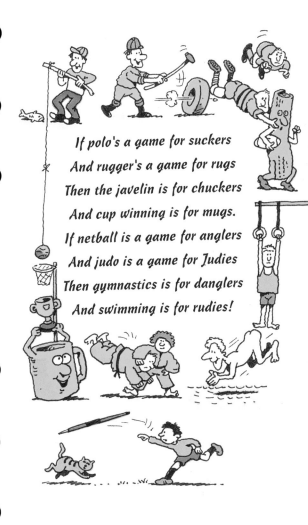

If polo's a game for suckers
And rugger's a game for rugs
Then the javelin is for chuckers
And cup winning is for mugs.
If netball is a game for anglers
And judo is a game for Judies
Then gymnastics is for danglers
And swimming is for rudies!

The horrors in Upper Form D
All went at the same time to pee.
Their teacher just stood
As they caused a huge flood
And the school floated off to the sea.

A Headteacher from France with large hands
Used to flap them and make strange demands.
But when these weren't met
He got in a fret
And wafted across to the Netherlands.

THE SCHOOL LIBRARY - SHHH!

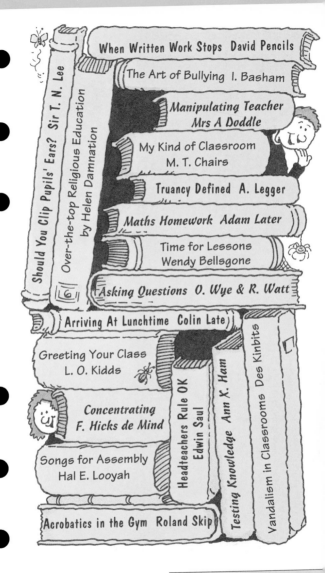

When Written Work Stops David Pencils

The Art of Bullying I. Basham

Manipulating Teacher
Mrs A Doddle

My Kind of Classroom
M. T. Chairs

Truancy Defined A. Legger

Maths Homework Adam Later

Time for Lessons
Wendy Bellsgone

Asking Questions O. Wye & R. Watt

Arriving At Lunchtime Colin Late

Should You Clip Pupils' Ears? Sir T. N. Lee

Over-the-top Religious Education
by Helen Damnation

Greeting Your Class
L. O. Kidds

Concentrating
F. Hicks de Mind

Songs for Assembly
Hal E. Looyah

Headteachers Rule OK
Edwin Saul

Testing Knowledge Ann X. Ham

Vandalism in Classrooms Des Kinbits

Acrobatics in the Gym Roland Skip

I WAS LATE FOR SCHOOL BECAUSE...

Someone had superglued the lid to the syrup tin and mum won't let me come out without breakfast.

I squeezed the toothpaste too hard, and it took ages to get it back into the tube.

I dreamed that the Headteacher had died and we were having a day of mourning.

Mum thought it was Sunday because dad took her out last night.

We were playing Blind Man's Buff in the playground and no-one told me the bell had gone.

I went to school with a load of kids. It was a high school - there were plenty of stairs. All the kids were good at archery because they had bow legs.

Nits were common, older people called them teachers. We used to pray before school dinners, then receive the last rites after we'd eaten them. Sometimes we'd have carrots, and other times we'd also have carrots.

Teachers were strict. They used so many canes that a jungle next to the school disappeared.

I left school at twelve to go down the mines - do I regret it? Yes, I wish I'd left the day I started.

Forenames: Cedric Edward
Born: Minehead
Educated: Edinburgh University
Former occupation: Head Gardener
Wife's name: Edwina
Home:
The Headquarters,
Hampstead
Favourite Place:
Garden shed
Holiday home: Edmonton
Drink: Red wine
Sports hero: Stefan Edberg
Actor: Eddie Murphy
Cricket ground: Headingley
Possessions: Coins
(half of them are heads)

BUT, SIR...

PARENT'S EVENING

THE LOW-DOWN ON TEACHERS

END OF TERM REPORTS

I'm sure Eve would not be stared at so much if she came to school with clothes on.

Buck is coming on by leaps and bounds.

After Gary was expelled, he became a joy to teach.

I do not expect Deborah to make any more progress this year. Mr Sykes - 1st January.

Your son has the ability to go places - I wish he would!

Your son would find a job in the building industry - as two short planks.

If your daughter behaved at home as she does at school, then I am certain you would have her adopted.

Your daughter never finishes things, largely because she never starts anything.

I'd send your child to boarding school - he is always bored.

WELL, I DON'T KNOW EITHER

PERFECT POEMS

A caretaker called old Mr Stowes
Caught kids hammering nails in his toes.
He's now so afraid
That more traps are laid
He takes pliers wherever he goes.

There was a young man from Japan,
Whose poetry just didn't scan.
One day when asked why,
He replied "'Cause I try
To fit as many words into the last
line as I possibly can."

CONDUCT AND PUNCTUALITY - D MINUS

Monday's dinner looked a treat
- a plate of crawling nits.
Tuesday's lunch I didn't eat
- the plate was glued in bits.
Wednesday's dinner looked like pie
that had been cooked in soap.
Thursday's lunch was an old school tie
and two strands of stale rope.
Friday's dinner was gungy-goo
and a welly filled with meat.
It's Saturday now, I've got the flu,
And I'm far too weak to eat.

DON'T YOU KNOW ANYTHING?

A gardening teacher from Leeds
Once swallowed a packet of seeds.
A big yellow rose
Grew out of his nose
And his beard was a tangle of weeds.

There was a student in Hong Kong,
Whose poems were always too long.
When asked why this was,
He said "It's because
Although I try hard, the last line always
seems to go on and
on and on..."

SPACE AGE SCHOOL

TEACHER KNOWS BEST - SOMETIMES

TEACHER TUNES

Sir is kind and Sir is gentle,
Sir is strong and Sir is mental.

Land of soapy water,
Teacher's having a bath.
Headmaster's looking through the keyhole,
Having a jolly good laugh.

Build a bonfire, build a bonfire
Put teacher on the top.
Put the headmaster in the middle
And burn the blummin' lot.

God made the bees,
The bees make the honey.
We do all the dirty work
The teachers make the money.

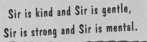

LAUGHABLE LITERATURE

Who wrote "Alice through the Cabbage Patch"? Lewis Carrot.

Who was the first prehistoric novelist? Charlotte Brontesaurus.

Who was the happiest writer of the 20th century? Graham Grin.

What detective writer was white and lacy? Sir Arthur Conan Doily.

Which children's author would you find in a flower bed? Roald Dahlia.

What novelist was a champion Subbuteo player? Charles Flickens.

PARENTS ARE AS BAD AS TEACHERS

I love to do my homework
It makes me feel so good.
I love to do exactly
As my teacher says I should.

I love to do my homework
I do it every day.
I even love the men in white
Who are taking me away.

Said a boy to his teacher one day,
"Wright has not written 'rite' right, I say."
And the teacher replied
As the error she eyed:
"Right! - Write 'rite' right, right away!"

PAY ATTENTION, PLEASE